THE ROMAN NUMERALS

MATH BOOK 6ᵗʰ GRADE

Children's Math Books

BABY PROFESSOR
EDUCATION KIDS

Speedy Publishing LLC
40 E. Main St. #1156
Newark, DE 19711
www.speedypublishing.com

LET'S START COUNTING WITH ROMAN NUMERALS

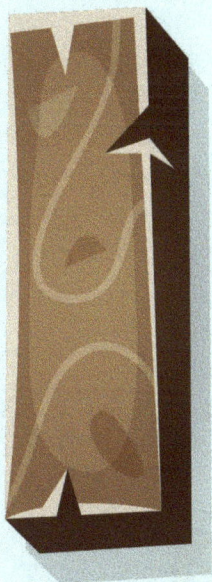

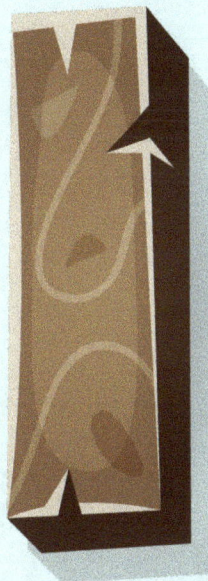

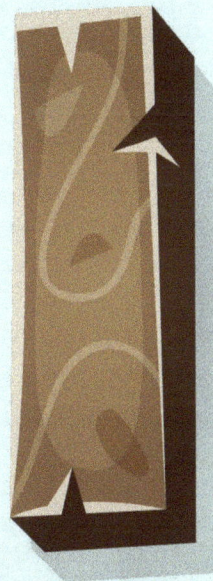

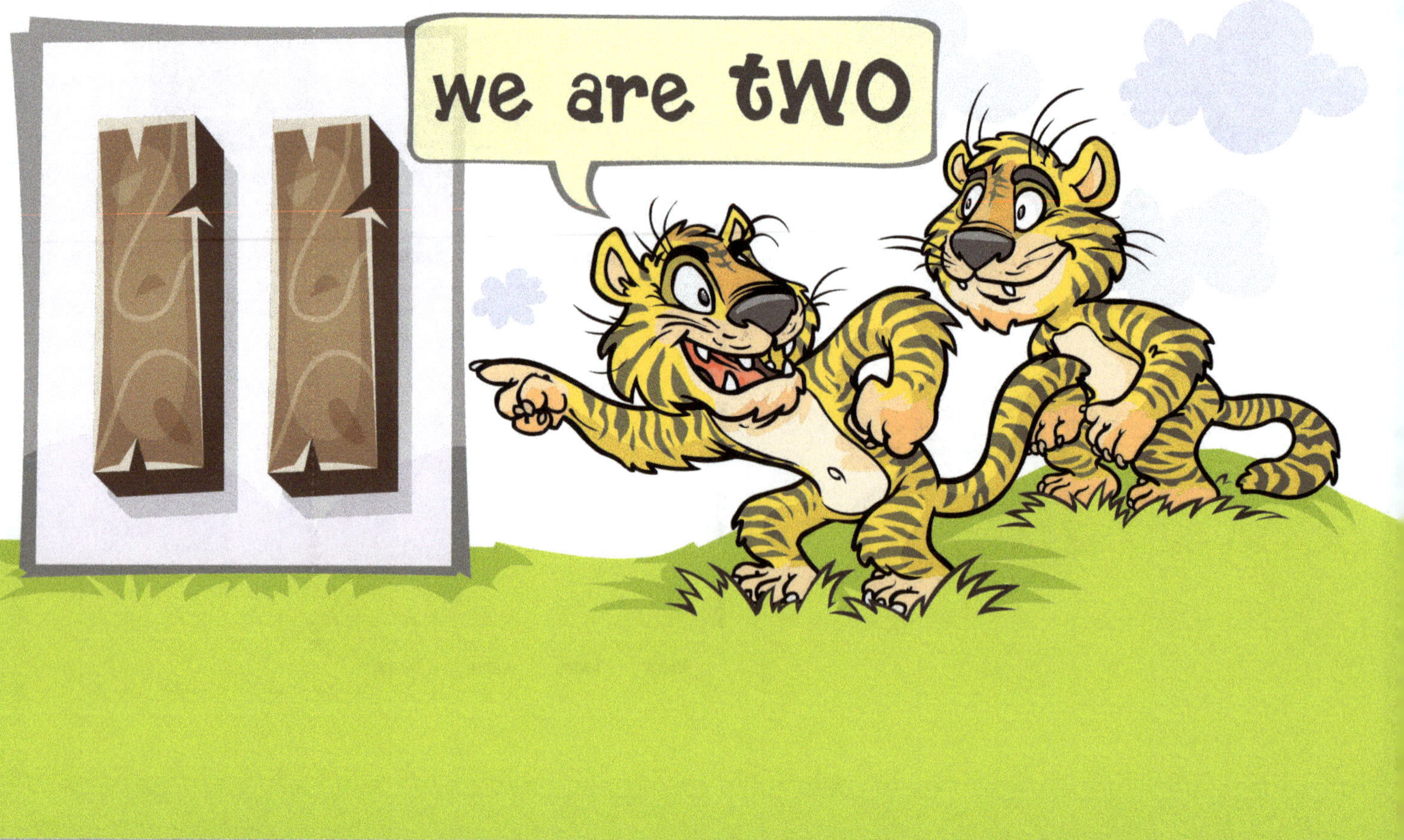
we are two

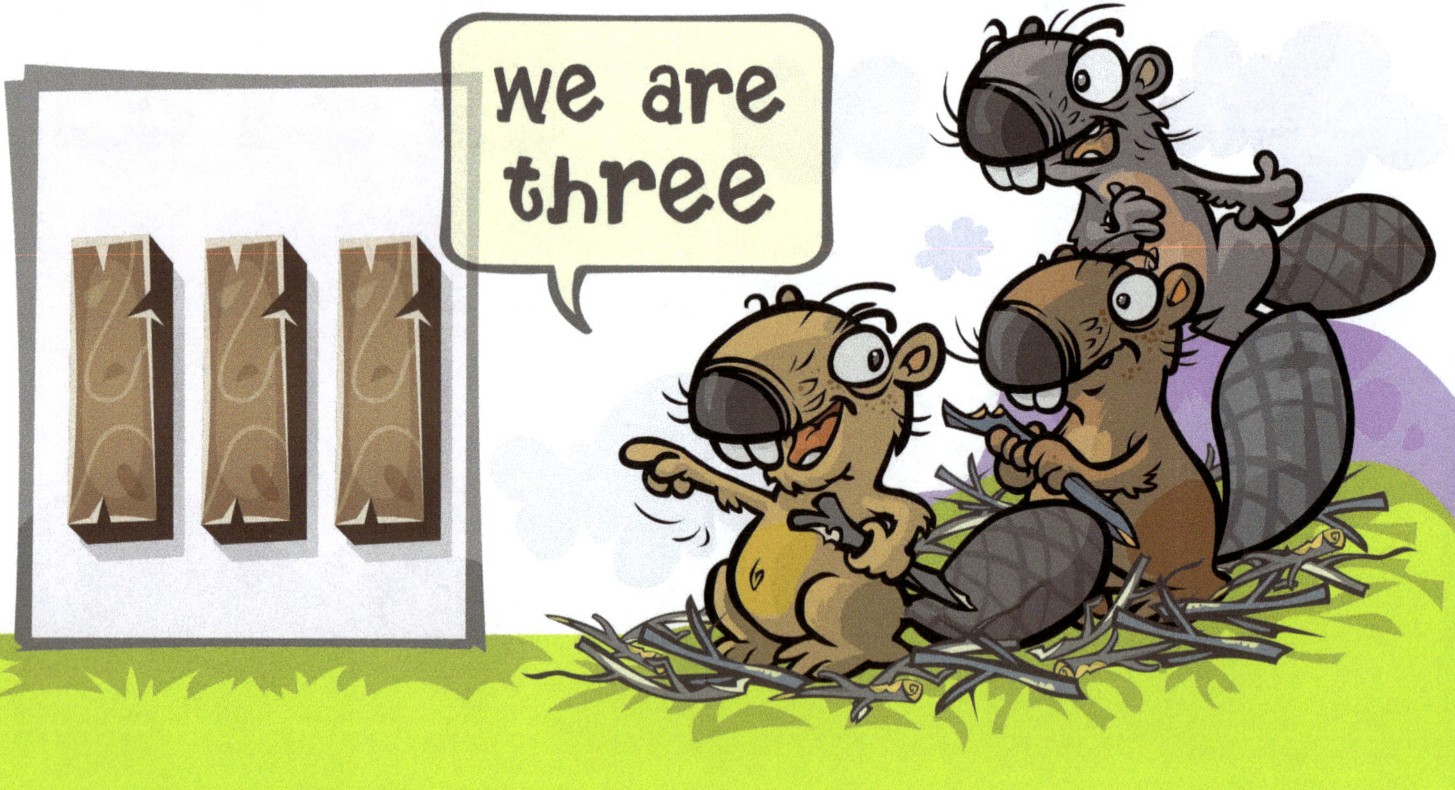
we are
three

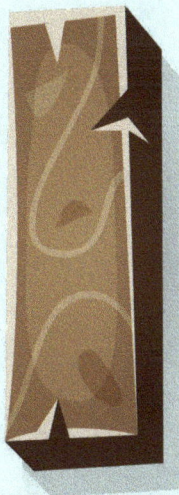 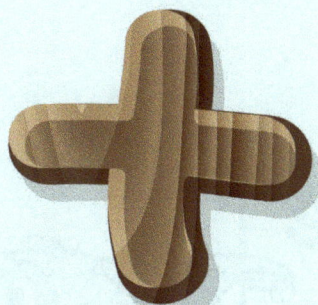 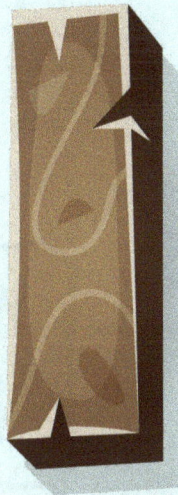 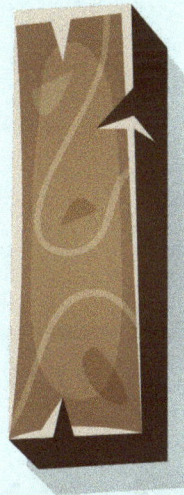

VI - II

=

we are
eight

VIII

  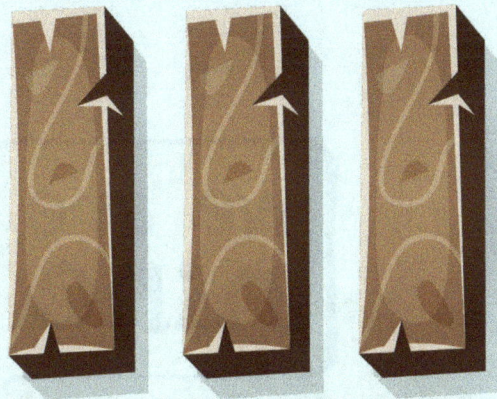

ten

XI

eleven

XII

twelve

XIII

thirteen

XIV

fourteen

XV

fifteen

XVI

sixteen

XVII

seventeen

XVIII

eighteen

XIX

nineteen

X X

twenty

XXX

thirty

L − X = [?]

XL

forty

L

fifty

LX

sixty

LXX

seventy

LXXX

eighty

C - X = ?

XC

ninety

one hundred

two hundred

CCC

three hundred

D - C = [?]

CD

four hundred

five hundred

DC

six hundred

DCC

seven hundred

DCCC

eight hundred

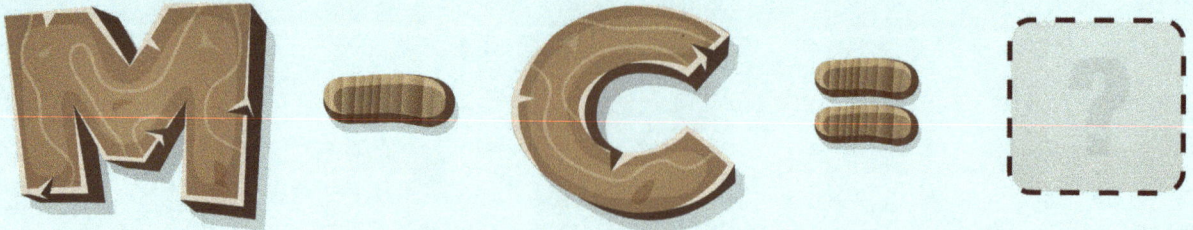

M - C = [?]

CM

nine hundred

one thousand

two thousand

MMM

three thousand

MMMM

four thousand

The dash above the Roman numeral is used to indicate that the number under the dash is to be multiplied by 1,000. It is also known as the Vinculum.

five thousand

ten thousand

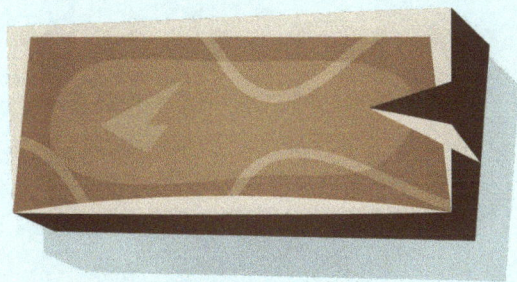

fifty thousand

one hundred thousand

five hundred thousand

ANSWERS

1.  O

2. I

3. 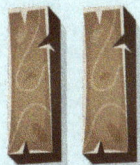 II

4. 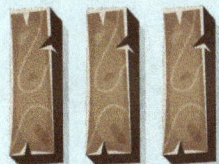 III

5.  IV

6.  VI

7.  VII

8.  VIII

9.  IX

10.  X

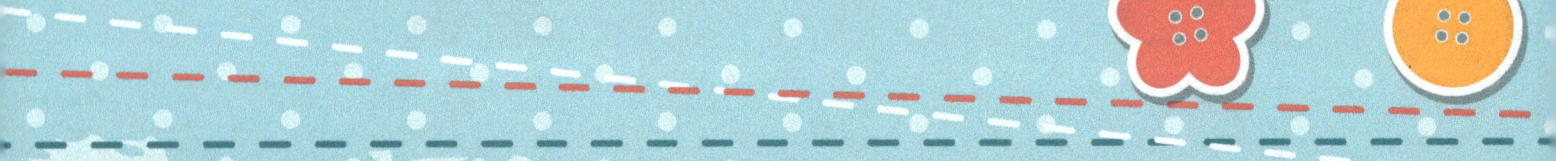

Visit

BABY PROFESSOR
EDUCATION KIDS

www.BabyProfessorBooks.com

to download Free Baby Professor eBooks
and view our catalog of new and exciting
Children's Books

Milton Keynes UK
Ingram Content Group UK Ltd.
UKHW051709030924
447642UK00002BA/155